# SERMON

ON THE COMPLETION OF

# THE ATLANTIC TELEGRAPH.

Mrs Zechariah Allen,
with the writer's affec^e regards.

# A
# SERMON

ADDRESSED TO THE

SECOND PRESBYTERIAN CONGREGATION, ALBANY,

ON SUNDAY MORNING, SEPTEMBER 5, 1858,

ON THE COMPLETION OF

# THE ATLANTIC TELEGRAPH.

BY WILLIAM B. SPRAGUE, D. D.,

THEIR PASTOR.

---

PUBLISHED BY REQUEST OF THE YOUNG MEN OF THE CONGREGATION.

---

ALBANY:
CHARLES VAN BENTHUYSEN.
1858.

TO

# J. K. PORTER, ESQ.,

AND NINETY-SIX OTHERS,

MEMBERS OF THE SECOND PRESBYTERIAN CONGREGATION,

AND NEARLY ALL YOUNG MEN,

WHO HAVE ASSOCIATED IN THE REQUEST THAT THIS DISCOURSE MIGHT

BE PUBLISHED, IT IS NOW

RESPECTFULLY AND AFFECTIONATELY INSCRIBED,

WITH AN EARNEST WISH THAT THEIR HAPPINESS AND USEFULNESS

MAY BE INCREASED, AS THE HAND OF PROVIDENCE AND

THE RESEARCHES OF SCIENCE ARE SUPPLYING

NEW HELPERS TO BOTH;

AND THAT WHEN THE ELECTRIC TELEGRAPH SHALL HAVE

FULFILLED ITS MISSION, THEY MAY HAVE ONLY BEGUN THEIRS, AS

"KINGS AND PRIESTS UNTO GOD."

W. B. S.

# SERMON.

PSALM LXXVII, 19.

THY WAY IS IN THE SEA.

It is interesting to notice how the providence of God, in its gradual developments, gives to many portions of the word of God a depth and breadth of meaning, which the writers themselves had never conceived of. It is impossible to say to what extent the Prophets understood many of their own predictions; but there is no doubt that when viewed, as we are permitted to view them, in the light of Christianity, and of History, and in connection with those great movements of Providence in which we recognise the signs of the times, they widen and brighten into something far more extended and impressive than ever entered the minds to which they were originally communicated. And the same is true of other portions of Scripture—though they had a definite and important meaning when they were written, yet the progress of ages has been constantly adding to their import, or at least supplying new, and what would have seemed beforehand, most improbable, illustrations.

An example of this, if I mistake not, occurs in our text. The Psalmist, with a view to fortify himself against a desponding spirit, calls to remembrance not only the grace and faithfulness of God; but his almighty power and infinite majesty, especially as displayed in his deliverance of Israel from their Egyptian bondage. "Thy way is in the sea"—This expression no doubt refers to the miraculous opening of the Red Sea for the passage of the Israelites—the laws of nature, in obedience to Him who established them, were suspended—the bed of the sea was bared, and the waters were piled up like mountains on either side; and thus was formed the way by which God led his chosen people. But this allusion had a more general and much grander significance. It was designed to illustrate the depths of the Divine wisdom, the mysteriousness of the Divine movements; and wherever we pause,—whether amidst the works of creation or the works of providence, whether in the light of science or the light of Christianity,—as soon as we begin to meditate and inquire, we find ourselves on the borders of a vast region of unrevealed mystery.

Need I say that this passage has not only a figurative but literal illustration in that wonder of the age, before which the whole world is bowing in reverent amazement; in honour of which we have just kept a jubilee which cast into the shade our glorious Fourth, inasmuch as the one has a mere national bearing, while the other embraces the interests of our universal humanity. When we think that a principle has been discovered, and a work accomplished, by means of which human thought flashes in lightning all through the ocean's depths, and we converse with those who live on the other side of the globe almost as if they and we occupied adjoining habitations, well may we lift up our hearts to the wonder-working God, and exclaim,—"*Thy* way is in the sea." *Thou* hast ordained that wonderful law of the creation, which has its operation in this stupendous achievement. *Thou* hast smiled on the researches of science, thus rendering it successful to the discovery and the application of this law. *Thou* hast, by thy favouring providence, brought the enterprise to a brilliant consummation. And now we would reverently recognise this new way, opened at the bottom of the sea, as *thy* way. We would meditate upon it with humble docility. Not for purposes of mere lofty speculation, or intellectual indulgence, or fruitless wonder, but to get our minds filled with nobler thoughts of God, and our hearts with more reverent and devout affections towards Him, and to get the spirit of obedience and submission to his will more thoroughly infused into our lives, would we hold this last, this grandest of all human discoveries to our minds, in connection with the public services of the Sabbath day. Surely it is no desecration of holy time to honour God in his works; especially to take solemn and reverential note of that which marks an epoch, I might almost say, in the unfolding of the Divine perfections.

I. Here then, in the first place, let us learn a lesson *not only of the manifestation, but of the hiding, of God's power.*

Our highest idea of the power of God is gathered, not from abstract speculation on the infinity of the Divine nature, but from the actual effects produced by that power, as they come within the range of our own observation. He who looks at the works of God with an untutored mind, whose eye has never been taught to penetrate beneath the surface of any thing, and who knows as little of the laws of creation, as can consist with his having a place in it,—even *he* is overwhelmed, according to his humble measure, by thinking of the power that built the mountains, and spread the seas, and garnished the skies, and framed the innumerable glories which he beholds around him. But how much brighter and loftier must *his* conceptions of the Divine power be, who looks at these same works with an eye that has been schooled by science and philosophy; who looks at the heavens as an astronomer and at the earth as a geologist; and sees the operation of unvarying and harmonious laws, where another would see nothing beyond the mere succession or recurrence of events. And we shall not reach the highest idea of God's power in creation, by contemplating the creation as the *product* of his power, unless we look also at the energy which He has *imparted* to his works. We must mark the various intellectual, moral and physical forces which are lodged in them; must bear in mind that the angels who excel in strength, derive all their strength from Him; that He gives power to mortals to train, I had almost said to domesticate, his own lightning; that He gives power to the ocean, now to bear the great ships majestically on its bosom, and now to lash itself into a fury, that seems to threaten the very heavens. Oh yes, if you will gain any thing like an adequate idea of God's Omnipotence as displayed in his works, you must contemplate the power which He has actually infused into them: in the vastness, the grandeur, the energy of their operations, you must recognise not merely the laws by which they are controlled, but the workings of God's own almighty hand. In short, you must remember that all the power that is displayed or exercised in the Universe, is but an emanation from Omnipotence.

It is one of the tendencies of habit to impair our sense of the force of evidence, and make us indifferent to the teachings of wisdom. Ever since we opened our eyes upon the light, we have been living in a world where every object has been preaching to us of the mighty power of God. The sun has been shining by day and the moon and the stars by night; the mountains, piercing the clouds, have been standing firm on their bases; the old ocean has been perpetually heaving in restless grandeur; the whole course of nature has been going forward with ceaseless regularity,—all, all have been speaking to us of God's mighty power; and yet, even in such a school as this, how little have we really learned of this momentous subject—or I should rather say, how little have we been impressed by that which we could not fail to acknowledge! Now I do not undertake to say that the recent discovery or achievement which is filling the world with wonder, gives us a higher idea of the Divine power than is to be gathered from other of God's ordinances in the kingdom of nature; but the fact that this discovery is new, gives to it, in respect to ourselves, the force of a fresh revelation. We look at the heavenly orbs performing their courses with undeviating exactness; we experience the regular changes of the seasons and the succession of day and night, and our only reflection perhaps is that all these things are as they have always been. But when we stand on one side of the ocean, and convey not only our thoughts but our words distinctly to the other side of it, without the intervention of a moment; we recognise a new agency here that startles and overwhelms us. The blinding influence of sense and habit ceases to be felt; and instead of giving a mere cold and formal assent to the truth that God is Omnipotent, this truth settles upon our spirits as a living and mighty reality.

But I have said that the recent triumph in the world of science suggests to us the *hiding* as well as the manifestation of God's power. To have created and fixed those mighty forces on which has depended this wonderful result, involves an exercise of power which indeed baffles our highest conceptions. But who shall say that this is the *limit* of the almighty power of God? Who can assure us that in the progress of ages there shall not be other manifestations of this attribute, that, even to those who stand nearest the throne, shall seem to overshadow the grandest exercise of it which they had known before? Who can say but that even before these heavens and this earth shall give place to the new heavens and the new earth, the hand of the Almighty may be revealed even here, in changes such as have had no parallel in the previous history of the race? Believe me, when you have formed your highest conceptions of Divine power from what you see, you have only entered the vestibule of infinity; and that period in your existence will never come, when there will not be unmeasured, fathomless depths, from which, even though you were transformed into an angel, you could only retire with the self-abasing exclamation,—"Who can find out the Almighty unto perfection!"

But the power of God does not exist as an insulated attribute—and it becomes an object of terror or of joy, as it is associated in the mind of the sinner with justice, in the mind of the saint with mercy. The sinner has put himself in an attitude of rebellion against God; and rebellion is a capital offence—it is a direct assault upon all the great interests of Jehovah's Kingdom—the punishment threatened is eternal death; and that which God's justice has decreed, his power will inevitably execute.

But the Christian, who has entered into covenant with God, and thus become entitled, according to the Divine constitution, to the merciful provisions of the Gospel, has this same almighty power pledged for his perfect safety, his final and everlasting triumph. The sinner may surround himself with the glare of worldly greatness; he may have vast possessions; he may wield an iron sceptre; and his influence may seem almost as wide as the world itself; but yet he is as truly within the range of the Divine power as is the most abject slave that wears a chain, or the meanest reptile that creeps upon the earth. The saint may be an exile not only from the world's luxuries but from the world's comforts; he may be the object not only of poverty but of reproach and persecution; and at the end of life's pilgrimage, he may find the martyr's stake waiting for him; and yet in all this God's almighty power is working for his highest good; it puts love and blessing even into what seemed a ministration of wrath and wo; it is the pledge that the sower in tears shall be the reaper in joy. Let not the prosperous sinner then be deluded by his fancied triumph; neither let the afflicted

Christian be discouraged by his manifold trials; for as sure as God's word is truth and his arm is power, so sure shall the triumph of the former be turned into shame, and the trials of the latter issue in the exceeding and eternal weight of glory.

II. This new way which has been opened in the sea, suggests to us *the greatness or the littleness of the human intellect, according to the standpoint from which it is viewed.*

Man, though he is not the noblest, is yet far from being the meanest, of God's creatures. If on one side of him are the beasts that perish, on the other side are the angels who minister before God's throne; and if he is materially allied to the former, though much above them, he is intellectually allied to the latter, though much below them. We are not to judge of the capacities of the human mind from the humble measure of intelligence and culture that ordinarily obtains among men; for the multitude are, by the very law of their earthly condition, kept from making high attainments; but we are to judge of it rather from those rare cases in which Nature has been bountiful of her gifts, and Providence of her advantages; in which the mind has asserted its native dignity in some grand achievement, that has served to put to shame the efforts of all other minds in the same direction. Newton, and Bacon, and Boyle, and Locke, and Edwards, and Franklin, and Fulton,—how each of them led the way into unexplored regions of thought, and built for himself a monument that bids defiance to all the ages. And now here is another grand result from the labours of science ; and whether it be viewed absolutely, or in comparison with the ordinary standard of intellectual development, is it not fitted to exalt our conceptions of the capabilities of our own nature? Does it not help to redeem man from the insignificance to which the grovelling tastes and habits of the multitude would seem to degrade him, and lift him towards that position which he may legitimately claim, as having been made *a little* lower than the angels?

And who can estimate the responsibility that pertains to the possession of such a nature? Hast thou ever reflected seriously on what it is to be a man; to have a principle within thee that is capable of measuring the distances of the stars, and sending thought down into the caverns of the ocean? Take heed that thou dost not undervalue thyself; that thou dost not waste these noble powers upon unworthy objects; that, instead of aspiring to share the society and employments of angels, thou dost not content thyself to sink to the level of brutes. Cultivate thine intellect as far as God gives thee opportunity; but, above all, see that its faculties are kept in strict subjection to the Divine will, and rendered subservient to the Divine glory. Thou hast within thee that which may make thee a very angel at last—how fearful the thought that neglect, perversion, may plunge thee into everlasting shame and contempt!

But suppose that, instead of comparing man with the orders of creation below him, or the loftiest human intellect with the meanest, we compare the greatest human mind with the infinite and the unsearchable; and suppose that, instead of comparing the ground that has already been gained in the great field of knowledge with the barbarism of the darkest age, we compare it with the immeasurable region that is yet before us, and which none but God

Himself can fully explore—how essentially does man become reduced in his intellectual stature—how the majesty of his nature degenerates into insignificance, and its strength into weakness, and we are led almost to ignore the nobility which actually pertains to him. Let the recent discovery be an illustration. It is indeed one of the noblest triumphs both of science and of art; and when we look at it either as a bright and startling wonder, or as a contribution to the stock of human knowledge, or as a new element in the world's civilization, we cannot but pause in admiration of the mighty *human* power by which it has been accomplished. But what, after all, is here the extent of man's doings? Man has only ascertained the existence of one of the laws of the creation; has only found out a new use of the electric fire; has only put in operation a hidden agency that has existed ever since the morning stars sang together. Let man be inquired of in respect to any thing beyond the simple law that is here brought into exercise, beyond the simple fact that has here been reached; let him be asked how or why the lightning not only becomes vocal, but makes this submarine passage, in obedience to the human will, and the prince of philosophers is no wiser to answer than the savage whose mind is as dark as the wilderness he inhabits. We do not suppose that this brilliant enterprise marks the *limit* of the mind's developments; but no matter what more glorious things there may be to come, it will never reach a point where the known will be to the unknown so much as a grain of sand is to the globe. There will always be stretching before it regions of thought which it has never explored; and each fresh attainment, instead of marking a resting place for the mind, will be a glimpse into the distant and untravelled future, to quicken it to higher aspirations and more vigorous efforts.

Shall not man then be abased before his Maker, even in view of the most signal of his triumphs? To say nothing here of his moral estrangement from God,—nothing of the degradation and ruin which sin has brought upon him,—is there not enough to bow his spirit in humility in the reflection that his faculties can grasp so little, that the limit of his knowledge is so quickly reached? If he is conscious of the rising of a spirit of self-exaltation, as he sits at his leisure, and puts God's messenger in requisition to do his work on another continent, surely that spirit may well find a check, and the opposite spirit of lowliness be brought into exercise, by the thought that his philosophy of the subject terminates with the fact, and that there is not one of the attending phenomena which he is able to explain.

III. This mysterious passage of the lightning through the sea *marks a bright epoch in the history of the world's progress.*

Progressive development seems to be the law of God's universal kingdom. This remark applies with peculiar force to the kingdom of grace,—whether in regard to the outward communication of Divine truth, or the inward experience of its power. From the first revelation that God made to the parents of our race, down to the last that was made to the beloved disciple on Patmos, the light gradually shone brighter through the Patriarchal, and Mosaic, until it finally reached its brightest splendour in the Christian, dispensation. So also the principle of Divine grace in the heart is at first only as a grain of mustard seed,—the smallest of all seeds; but it germinates into a tree of vigorous growth, which strikes its roots deep, and spreads abroad its branches, and gives forth its pleasant fruits with ever increasing luxuriance, until it finally becomes fit to be transplanted to the upper Paradise.

And if from the domain of religion we pass to that of civilization, we find the same principle constantly illustrated. Not indeed that the progress has been uniform from year to year, or that the human mind has not sometimes yielded to an ignoble repose, so that for a season the movement has seemed retrograde; but, on the whole, its march has been onward. It is worthy of notice that the progressive civilization of the world has been marked by distinct stages; that the discovery of one of the laws of nature, while it has led to great immediate results, has made way for the discovery in due time of another; and that each successive point that is reached, though the glory of it may be connected with a single name, is really the result of the accumulated intellectual forces of the age. Witness the discovery of the magnetic needle—what a mighty change did that work in human affairs—how it gave not only wings but security to commerce, and became a light to guide the mariner all over the dark ocean! The art of printing,—what an impulse did that give to the human mind,—not only waking up its energies, but conferring a sort of omnipresence upon its thoughts! The power of steam,—what has not that done in annihilating distances both by land and by water; in facilitating the accomplishment of men's plans, and quickening the spirit of public enterprise! And now, after the lapse of little more than half a century, comes yet another and still loftier development, in the flying of human thought not only through the air but beneath the ocean, in a way which utterly mocks our comprehension. This wonder of wonders is not yet old enough to enable us even to conjecture what must be its remoter results; but we surely cannot give to it a thought without perceiving that it must mark a mighty stride not only in the intellectual, but the moral and Christian, regeneration of the race. And while it is itself such a prodigious step onward, and is fraught with so much blessing, let it be remembered that it is a vast addition to the intellectual strength, or I should rather say, the intellectual *capital* of the world; that it furnishes a loftier eminence than has before been obtained, from which man may reach out and grasp the hidden wonders of immensity.

IV. And this leads me to say, in the last place, *what a wonderful bearing has the recent discovery upon the future!*

Who can estimate the effect which it must have in enlarging the stock of human knowledge, and quickening the march of general improvement? For many ages, such were the barriers to intercourse between the different nations, that it took a long time for a bright thought to travel over the world; and such a thing as the communion and co-operation of great minds on opposite sides of the globe was scarcely dreamed of. Since the wonder-working power of steam has become known, an important change in this respect has been effected; but it was left to the agency of electricity to complete the triumph. And now that the oceanic telegraph has proved a successful experiment, I might almost say that the last barrier to a universal intercourse is removed; and not a grand or brilliant or useful conception can be originated by a mind, even in the most distant country, but it comes darting to us, and goes darting all over the world, in all its freshness and power. Thus it is that men will be able at once to avail themselves of each other's intellectual labours; and the great stock of human knowledge will be increasing with a rapidity unknown to preceding ages. Thus the intellectual power of the world will quickly be concentrated, and the world itself will become a vast school, in which its brightest and most accomplished minds will, as if sitting together in one grand convocation, alternately impart and receive of their collected treasures.

And not only may we expect that this great event will minister to the intellectual advancement of the race, but we have reason to anticipate, as another result, a closer fellowship among the nations, and a more vigorous and effective co-operation for national and universal peace. It is hard for an individual to take the attitude of hostility towards one with whom he is on terms of constant intercourse; and the danger of his doing this is not a little diminished by the fact that such intercourse secures to him the opportunity of making or receiving explanatory or conciliatory statements. And the remark applies equally to nations as to individuals. There is no time now for misunderstanding to ripen into prejudice or hate, or for party rancour to breathe its venom throughout the length and breadth of a country, before an explanation can be communicated or received, that may effectually annihilate the supposed offence. Neither Great Britain nor America need to sleep a single night over any international matter that is even of doubtful import; for the ever faithful wires may always be put in requisition to ask or to convey the desired intelligence. Is it too much to expect that the disturbances among the nations, especially in their relations to each other, will henceforth be greatly diminished; and that each will realize the feelings of a common brotherhood to an extent hitherto unknown? Nay, is it presumptuous to hope that the fact that the first message that was brought to us through this strange channel, was that a fearful and protracted war had closed, may prove ominous of what is hereafter to be; and that we may recognise in the Atlantic telegraph not less an agent for the preservation of peace, than a means of spreading the goodly tidings of its existence?

But that which we may well regard as the climax, the consummation, of blessings connected with this enterprise, is its prospective influence on the evangelization and moral renovation of the world. The fact that it is likely to prove favourable to the *peace* of the nations, is an omen of much good in this respect; for while the Gospel itself is a message of peace and good-will to men, there is nothing so adverse to its reception as pre-existing national hostility; nothing so favourable to its reception as the absence of war, and tumult, and party strife, and the presence of that spirit that pays due respect to the rights and feelings of the common humanity. Hence we have reason to hope that the telegraph, in its more general operations in promoting a goodly fellowship between the inhabitants of different countries, will form the legitimate preparation for a more direct intercourse in reference to the interests of the Kingdom of Christ. Is there not a chord strung in the bosom of every true

Christian, that vibrates to the tidings of Zion's weal or wo, though coming even from the ends of the earth? Does not the principle of grace in the heart attain to a more vigorous life, from being brought into communion with the same principle in other hearts,—no matter by what instrumentality? What Christian is there who could hear that yesterday there was a meeting in London where a Pentecostal season was enjoyed, and thousands upon thousands, as in the days of Whitefield, were trembling under the sense of sin, or rejoicing in the hope of forgiveness; or that, day before yesterday, there was a meeting in Paris, or even in Rome, beneath the very shadow of the Vatican, at which Romanism herself stood abashed at the manifest presence and power of God's Spirit;—what Christian, I say, could hear such intelligence, without being quickened to a higher tone of feeling and of effort; without giving himself anew to that cause which is thus rising and triumphing among the nations? And no doubt there will be many other ways in which Christianity will be helped forward by this same instrumentality. Indeed it requires no great stretch of imagination to suppose that these wires that pass through the ocean, may ultimately be rendered even more subservient to sacred than to secular purposes; and that when the millenial day shall spread its glories over the earth, this mysterious agent may be found to be closely allied to that angel that was seen flying through Heaven, having the everlasting Gospel to preach to every kindred, and nation, and tongue, and people.

If I mistake not, this grand discovery, in order to be duly estimated in its bearing on the Kingdom of Christ, must be viewed in connection with other things which give character to the day through which we are passing. What means the waking up, in so great a degree, of evangelical Christendom to the obligation of giving the Gospel to every creature? What means the casting away by Providence of those barriers of ages upon ages, which have kept the nations apart from each other, and which have rendered Paganism, in many instances, as inaccessible as she has been terrific? What means that great baptism of the Holy Ghost and of fire, which has lately pervaded our land, and has already added so much to Zion's beauty and strength? What means the far extended Union Prayer Meeting, which makes each Christian sect forgetful of its own shibboleth, and by the harmony not less than the fervour of its offerings, gives us a precious foretaste of the Millenium, and of Heaven? And, I may add, what was the import of the recent shocks and convulsions in the commercial world, which, for the time, left multitudes little else to do than stand still and gaze upon the ruin of their fortunes and their hopes? I tell you, my friends, the meaning of all this is, that God has begun to do a great work for his Church,—great I mean in comparison even with what he has done before; and here he has introduced a new agent for carrying it forward. Under the direction of his providence, there is a grand system of means now in operation, which cannot long advance with its present constantly accumulating energy, but that songs of thanksgiving will ascend from earth to Heaven, because the Kingdom of God has fully come.

Is it a mere fancy to imagine that this yoking of God's love with his lightning,—this employing of the swiftest of all his messengers to proclaim the triumphs of his Gospel, may be regarded as emblematical of the increased rapidity with which Christianity is to fulfil her high mission of circling the globe? I do not pretend to say what drawbacks may yet be revealed to us in the great work of moral renovation; or to what extent the Church may become oblivious of her dependance, and require to be schooled by affliction before she is prepared to enjoy a complete triumph. But if the Church is faithful to her high trust, there is every thing in the aspects of providence to indicate that the days of Satan's reign will soon be numbered; that idolatry and supersti-tion, error and crime, having lived out their little day of triumph in this redeemed world, will be driven into everlasting exile. Standing as you do, Brethren, on this lofty eminence, and looking out upon the world from amidst this profusion of Divine influences and Divine wonders, where even Nature herself, in a new and glorious form, is enlisting as a volunteer servant of the Most High, shall not your faith and your zeal, the tone of your spirit and the tone of your efforts, be greatly quickened, to help forward this grandest of all enterprises,—the Redeemer's universal reign.

But I must not close without suggesting a solemn caution. You do well to rejoice in this new epoch in the world's history; and it was fitting that you should testify your joy by appropriate demonstrations. I have nothing to say against the imposing grandeur and splendour of the other night, considered as a token of your high estimate of the blessing which God has hereby bestowed upon men. But I may not omit to remind you that you have individual interests to be cared for, of infinitely greater moment than all the combined results of science, superadded to all the riches and glory of the world. If you have never yet bowed personally to the claims of the Gospel,—no matter what inferior homage you may render to it,—then you have nothing to hope from the gracious provision which it offers, you have every thing to fear from the terrible woes which it reveals. There is admonition hanging even upon this bright discovery; for though God permits his creatures to use his lightning as a new medium of intercourse, yet He Himself sometimes uses it to blast and to consume; and thus, while in the former case it speaks to us of his love, in the latter it becomes a fearful representative of his justice. Wherefore, venture not to trifle with the Creator and the Ruler of the world. Think not to substitute admiration of his works for obedience to his laws. Let your whole soul be concentrated upon the one great point of becoming a new creature in Christ Jesus. Kneel penitently at the mercy seat; lift a believing eye to the Cross; enter the straight, the narrow, the upward path; and then each successive discovery in the kingdom of nature will become with you a new element of devotion, a fresh token of Divine love, a pledge of the infinitely nobler discoveries that shall reward your admiring scrutiny beyond the vail.

www.ingramcontent.com/pod-product-compliance
Lightning Source LLC
LaVergne TN
LVHW011124110826
845150LV00008B/2242

* 9 7 8 1 4 1 8 1 9 4 9 4 9 *